A wise person once said to me, "The way to approach a problem is through the eyes of a person who has solved it." Mary Brite faced tragedy in her life— the stunning, breathtaking kind that is hardest to bear because it is most unexpected. . . .

The key to the story, of course, is her full and solid commitment to Jesus Christ. She got past the verbiage and the superficiality of much talk and experienced the truth as it really is.

I take pleasure in encouraging you to read on. You will be a better person for doing so.

—Sherwood Eliot Wirt

This book represents the top selection by the judges of the Warner Press 1975 Book Award Contest, the best of more than 400 entrants.

Both Warner Press and Pillar Books are proud to bring this effective and inspiring story to the widest possible audience.

TOP
OF THE
VALLEY

Mary Brite

PILLAR BOOKS NEW YORK

TOP OF THE VALLEY

A PILLAR BOOK

Pillar Books edition published February 1976

ISBN: 0-89129-087-7

Copyright © 1976 by Warner Press, Inc.

Printed in the United States of America

PILLAR BOOKS is a division of Pyramid Communications, Inc. 919 Third Avenue, New York, New York 10022 U.S.A.

This book is lovingly dedicated

to my parents

Leo and Bessie Bowers

who demonstrate faith in the Lord God

themselves

others

and me.

And for my soul-mate:

my gratitude

for walking the second mile.

Preface

A wise person once said to me, "The way to approach a problem is through the eyes of a person who has solved it." Mary Brite faced tragedy in her life—the stunning, breathtaking kind that is hardest to bear because it is most unexpected. Her resilience and resourcefulness in picking up the pieces of her life and putting them back together makes good reading.

The key to the story, of course, is her full and solid commitment to Jesus Christ. She got past the verbiage and the superficiality of much talk about Jesus and experienced the truth as it is in Christ.

I take pleasure in encouraging you to read on. You will be a better person for doing so.

—Sherwood Eliot Wirt

Part I

Yea, though I walk
through the valley of
the shadow of death . . .

There was nothing visible at twelve noon to indicate that my life would be shattered by twelve midnight on the first day of January, 1967. Clouds near Pike's Peak assisted the noonday sun in a game of peek-a-boo with a green and brown patchwork quilt of earth below.

A wave of love pulled me toward my husband Charlie, and warm desire spread through my body as his shy smile retained its power to make my heart hurry. My identity had been lost for years within his life goals but I didn't mind. I did envy his naturally tanned complexion as he stood on the church steps visiting with Don Beal, our youth minister.

"Hi, Don. How was the night?" Charlie asked. His attentive hazel eyes proved his genuine interest. I admired his broad shoulders and then pulled a loose button from his wool plaid jacket as I moved to stand near him.

"Fair, Dr. Venable. I finally got to sleep from four to six this morning," Don answered, rubbing his eyes.

Don wasn't tall in stature, but he lived on a pedestal

in the eyes of our children because of the church-related activities he planned with them. They had just completed an overnight retreat together.

"Could you see the fireworks near the top of Pike's Peak at midnight?" Charlie and I had watched this unique greeting from fellows in the Ad-a-Man Club who climbed the mountain each year.

"Part of them," Don said, as he wearily nodded his head.

"How is your wife?" Charlie asked.

"She's in Kansas visiting her parents. I'm going to drive down this afternoon to bring her and the baby home."

We walked to Don's car and helped our older son and daughter unload their sleeping bags.

"Can you stay awake for that long drive?" Charlie asked, as he helped load the bags into our car.

"I hope so," Don replied.

Charlie thanked him for the overnight care of Danny and Kathy. Ruthy and Paul David, our younger two children, came out of the church and our family of six rode home with the crisp air blowing in through the open car windows. Winter was rarely a lasting problem in Colorado Springs. Situated at the base of the mountains, the town was partially protected by Pike's Peak.

Charlie swung me up into his strong arms after we stepped inside our small kitchen and gave me a big hug.

"I really like that new red dress on you," he said as he held me closely. He rarely expressed verbal admiration or open affection, but when he did, it was always sincere. Fresh energy and excitement flooded my body. I squeezed him tightly, reluctant to let him go even as far as the clothes closet.

A kaleidoscope of colorful memories formed in my mind one after another—feeding Charlie a piece of our wedding cake from my hand; sounds of his deep chuckled laughter; Charlie and I singing music in duet; Charlie playing croquet with our children; and smile crinkles at the corners of his eyes just before his comfortable body held mine at night.

Always sentimental, I deposited the recent hug and compliment in my memory stream, gold to draw upon in the future. The new year seemed to be getting off to a fine beginning!

"Could I offer to pilot Don to Kansas to get his w and baby?" Charlie asked. "It's a great day for flying."

"I think it would be a fine idea," I replied.

I knew we were thinking in parallel as we both recalled a frightening automobile ride. We had been traveling home from a distance and hadn't rested well during previous nights. Nearly home, Charlie had fallen asleep driving.

"When I opened my eyes we were on the shoulder of the road, headed for the ditch. I didn't want to jerk the wheel too suddenly for fear the car would turn over. I reached a quick decision to allow it to continue its direction," he had explained afterward.

Over the edge of a six-foot drop and several yards further ahead we had bumped to an abrupt stop. We calmed our screaming children and were relieved to find no physical human injuries. The car had a broken rear axle though, so we walked the last mile home.

We were thinking that maybe Don wouldn't be so fortunate in his travels today as we had been years ago.

My mind returned to Charlie's question. The trip could serve two purposes. Charlie needed the relaxation. Flying was his hobby. Our living expenses com-

bined with the cost of beginning a dental practice within the past three years had made it necessary for him to
work beyond ordinary endurance. And I, of necessity,
had continued to teach school. We couldn't afford to
rent a plane often.

Charlie pushed a curl of dark hair up from his fore-
head as he spoke to Don on the telephone. "I'd like to
rent a plane and fly you to Kansas." I heard growing
enthusiasm in his quiet voice.

"Don says okay," Charlie turned and called to me.

"Tell him to come on over for lunch." I was slicing
st beef.

Charlie repeated my invitation into the telephone.
"We'll eat together and make plans during the meal,"
he said at the end of their conversation.

Then he dialed a rental plane service number and
made arrangements to use the usual Cessna 205, a six-
seater.

Next he questioned each child about going to Kansas.
Paul David, nine, shook his head of auburn hair. "Not
me. I get airsick!"

"I'm sleepy," Kathy said as she set the kitchen table
for lunch. "We talked all night." Could she finally be
overcoming her shyness? I pondered, pleased. I had
fallen in love with Charlie when I was her age, thirteen.

"I'm too tired," Danny called from the bedroom
where he and Paul David bunked. His voice broke and
changed octaves in the middle of the sentence. As he
returned to the living room I noticed his jeans were
getting too short again. We had called my brother a silo
when he was fifteen years old because of his big appetite and long legs. An apt description of Danny, too, I
thought.

Ruthy, eleven, always wanted to go with her daddy,

a feeling she and I shared. She was the only one of the four children eager to fly at the moment, though, so we'd have some extra space in the plane.

After lunch, Charlie called Burl, the bass soloist of our church choir. "Wo...

be back...

ti...

l...

...

perienc...

arrived...

flight...

each accomplishment during the sixteen years of our married life?

Flying, too? Or maybe everything except flying? Or was it that he felt so much more free in the air than ~~was in complete control~~ ... good osa feeling she and I shared. She was the only one of the four children eager to fly at the moment, though, so we'd have some extra space in the plane.

After lunch, Charlie called Burl, the bass soloist of our church choir. "Would you like to fly to Kansas and be back before dark?" I heard him ask. "You said one time you'd like to go along on any cross-country just for the ride, and we have an empty seat."

Burl accepted, looking forward positively to an experience that would have many negative aspects. He arrived at the airport before we did, carrying a large flight jacket to warm his six-foot-two form. He greeted us with his deep voice. "Hi! The weather looks great for flying!"

Ruthy and I climbed into the plane. We could hear the men visiting as they checked over the outer plane surface. Their voices were momentarily drowned out by a small plane rolling past us to the parking area.

I frequently waited while Burl and Charlie discussed flying after choir rehearsals on Thursday nights. Burl owned a small plane and had a private pilot's license, too.

Charlie, Burl, and Don climbed in and we all buckled our seat belts. Charlie followed proper procedure using a checklist before taking off a little later than planned. Ordinary problems were left below as we lifted and turned east, away from the mountains.

During the smooth flight time to Dighton I was surrounded by pleasant conversation, but my mind wandered into years past as I allowed myself to remember potential accidents—only briefly, for I felt I was showing a lack of trust in Charlie to think of them overmuch. Hadn't he spent extra hours and effort to perfect each accomplishment during the sixteen years of our married life?

Flying, too? Or maybe everything except flying? Or was it that he felt so much more free in the air than elsewhere that he thought he was in complete control and had grown careless? Act as usual, be a good ostrich, and bury your opinions in the sand, I cautioned myself.

Still, I couldn't help recalling a take-off in April, 1958. "We just narrowly cleared some trees," Charlie said right after we started to Oklahoma for the birth of Paul David.

I could hardly swallow, but didn't say anything.

"I knew our Piper PA-12 was overloaded, but I was determined to take off anyway," he said.

I was shocked, but didn't want to think about it so I purposely hid the doubt I felt. And I hadn't ever analyzed it, up to and including today. Nor had I totaled the hours it had taken me to learn to fly without fear.

Secondly, I thought back to a nearly disastrous night flight in May of 1965. It wasn't mandatory to be instrument-rated then and Charlie had enough experience flying at night that his parents, one sister, and I felt confident about beginning a trip to Oklahoma with him as pilot late in the evening.

In about an hour the plane deviated off course because Charlie had neglected to correct a change in direction. It was needed due to a crosswind. We lost the beep-beep sound of the Omni signal which directed us. We veered further off course as he attempted to compare an air map with landmarks below. Places were hard to identify in the dark with few lights to outline them.

Uneasiness filled the cabin. Where were we?

As Charlie searched the map the rest of us strained to see a lighted strip *anywhere* below in the darkness. We fought panic for thirty minutes, searching. Finally we saw a small lighted strip, circled, and landed. I could breathe normally again.

Charlie and his dad hurried out of the plane. They looked through a window into the small hangar and read a calendar on the wall.

"We are in Woodward, Oklahoma." Charlie said when they relaxed enough to climb back in beside us. "We could have been in Kansas or Texas."

Then we had taken off and flown straight to Stillwater, without any further trouble.

"Don't you dare take chances with the lives of others again, even if they are your relatives," I berated him later. I couldn't believe his actions, for they were so contrary to the way he usually lived.

Think of good things, I told myself and relived the peace of a Christmas vacation night in 1965 when we flew above a solid layer of clouds. The stars were bright and sparkling, looking near enough that I was tempted to reach out for them. The night sky was beautiful and suddenly I made a decision that it was too good to miss.

"This is where I want to be. If I die, I die," I had whispered.

God seemed close to me and my fear dropped below us. I began to understand Charlie's love of flying better after that experience, and I was relaxed and able to enjoy being in the air.

In spite of my attempt not to allow my mind to think negatively, I remembered that we had run out of gasoline trying to reach an alternate strip because of an unexpected ground blizzard as recently as March of 1966.

"Buckle your seat belts and put your faces in a pillow," Charlie had warned the children and me.

We landed in a cactus-covered pasture with scattered grazing cattle near us. It was Charlie's turn to be surprised for none of us showed any agitation.

"I thought you would panic," he said. "I'm proud of you."

"Why should we get hysterical? Haven't we practiced emergency landings?" I inquired quietly.

"Yes," he replied with wonder in his voice.

Think positive. Only three incidents in nine years of flying, I told myself.

I forced my thoughts back to the present and took an active part in the current conversation.

"Dighton coming up," I heard Don say to Charlie about an hour later.

When he sighted the airport Charlie circled once, and then a second time so he could see the wind soc more clearly. I glanced out the side window and saw that the dirt strip was dry, graded, and lined with snowy edges. Pastures nearby were patched with unmelted snow.

Don's wife and parents met us as the plane rolled to a stop. The men discussed altitude changes between Colorado and Kansas while we unloaded. Soon we were taken into a small, agricultural town to a parsonage. Don told us his father-in-law was minister of the church next door. We enjoyed getting acquainted with new friends while having coffee.

Soon, Charlie telephoned the nearest official and updated our flight plan. Then, for some unknown reason, he began to pace the floor. I had never seen him act in such a manner. He vocally wondered how far down the strip he could go before deciding if he would or would not definitely take off.

The sun was going down and he was still questioning as we drove back out to the airport in preparation for the return flight to Colorado Springs. I was getting restless. What was his concern?

"Could we drag the strip and look it over in the car before we take off?" Charlie asked. He seemed reluctant about taking off at all. He drove down the strip and back slowly and then faster.

Dusk was absorbing the evening shadows as we filled the baby's pink bathtub with diapers, clothes, and toys. Charlie placed it behind the back seat of the airplane.

"I believe I'll do a practice take-off and landing before I load all of you in," he said. He is thinking of my admonition to use care with the lives of others, I thought. Good . . . Burl followed him into the plane.

"My toes are getting numb. Let's go sit in the car and keep warm," I suggested. So the rest of us sat inside the car and watched.

"Charlie and Burl are looking over the instruments to be sure they are ready for take-off," I explained. Then the red and white plane moved down the strip, increased in speed near the end of the runway, and pulled up into the nearly dark sky.

We saw the plane lights clear the fence beside the highway, and lift above the red warning lights that topped the telephone poles.

Moving south and flashing steadily, the lights were swallowed into the earth on the first right turn.

"He's gone down!" The certainty of my feeling left me momentarily motionless.

"He's gone behind a hill over there," Don's father-in-law replied. We waited quietly a few minutes.

"A hill in flat Kansas?" Doubt and I met in a head-on scuffle.

We were in an area strange to me, but I couldn't accept the answer I was given. Still, I acted upon it outwardly, for I didn't want to upset Ruthy. I felt something was final about what we had just watched.

"I think he may have gone to the next town before coming back," Don answered. "He can get gasoline there."

I couldn't sit still. Don and I got out and walked around the car as if that act alone would make the plane return sooner. I couldn't remain quiet. "We don't *need* gasoline." I was positive Charlie and the plane had gone down so I pictured him injured and trying to get help.

"Maybe he is going to land on the black-top strip west of here and have us come there to take off instead of from this dirt strip." Don sounded reasonable.

"Is there a telephone here?" I looked around the darkening area. We found one on the wall outside the hangar, but it gulped the dime from my cold fingertips without a buzz.

"Let's go back into town so Charlie can call us," Don's father-in-law suggested from inside the warm car.

"I don't think we should leave," I said. But I could think of no reason to stay. It was the beginning of endless decision making. I was beginning to feel cold all over as we returned to the parsonage.

II

The plane had disappeared around 8:15 P.M.

I feared the worst. The organizational part of my mind began to take charge of my words and actions. "Is there a doctor in your church congregation?"

"Yes," replied Don's father-in-law.

"Would you please have him come and give Ruthy a sedative? I want her to sleep through all this." No one questioned my thinking. A doctor came and fed her pixie face a capsule.

I was aware of very little, but I do recall telling those around me that I had fallen in love with Charlie when I was very young and that we were married when I was nineteen. I remember saying that we had graduated from college in 1955 and that Charlie had graduated from college a second time, from dental school in 1964. I probably told them my whole life story even though I was feeling that nothing was real at the moment.

An hour passed. Remembering our three children at home, I called our family doctor and his wife. They were close friends. I told them where we were and what was happening. "Will you please go stay with Danny, Kathy, and David?" I asked. "They are home alone. Something is wrong, but we aren't sure what yet. And will you please send our minister over to stay with Burl's wife? We think Charlie and Burl may be down in the plane."

About 10:30 P.M. a man came to the living room where I waited. He questioned me about the plane size, if we owned or rented it, and if we had arrived with plenty of gasoline. None of us who had seen the plane take off thought to communicate the direction it had taken or the approximate distance it had gone so that he could inform those searching.

In the living room a clock struck midnight, but it had little meaning for me.

Around 1:00 A.M., five hours after Charlie had taken off, someone asked me if I would like to go to the search headquarters which had been set up in the church basement.

"Every farmer has gone out and checked his own land," a stranger there named George told us. "We started our organized search five miles west of town and are moving west. We have men from the Civil Air Patrol helping. Fellows from the next town west are walking east toward us."

"Five miles west of town? No wonder you aren't finding anything. Charlie didn't even *get* five miles west! Why did you start searching away out there?" I couldn't believe that hours had passed and nothing had been found.

"We had a farmer who telephoned a message that a light plane had flown over his house about 8:15, so we started the search on his land. He lives five miles west."

George explained their decision. It made sense to them, but not to me.

"Charlie didn't get that far. Will one of you drive me out to look for the plane?" I felt that a lot of time had been wasted.

"No," firmly, "You don't want to go out and look for the plane. We are trained for this."

"I must go look for Charlie." A strong inner force commanded me. I was positive I could find the plane, so I kept insisting.

"Okay, come on. I'll take you." George finally relented.

We walked out into the cold, dark night and left in his station wagon. We stopped on Main Street, while he purchased gasoline. A curious teen-aged boy climbed into the back seat.

While we sat in the car under the filling station lights and the fuel tank was being refilled, I drew a diagram in the dust on the car dashboard.

"If a plane took off here, beside the hangar, with the highway there, above it telephone lines with red lights on top, the railroad tracks nearby, and if the plane went south about a mile and a half—and crashed—where would it be?"

"You would be at the outdoor theater or the city dump," George replied.

"Okay. Those are the two places I want to go."

What irony—if Charlie, who worked so hard for perfection, ended up in a rubbish pile! What was happening?

We drove first to the theater area and looked around with a light that George plugged into the dash. He seemed to be prepared for this moonless night. There were several car tracks, but nothing significant.

We went back out to the highway and west again. We passed a dirt road that turned south. "Where is that road in relation to the two places you mentioned?" I asked.

"About halfway in between the two—" George slowed the car.

"Let's go down that road." A knowledge was unwavering within me. I don't know *how* I knew, just that I *did* know, although I had never been in this county before in my life.

A loose stone tossed by a tire hit the underside of the car. We drove slowly along a gravel road about a mile and a half. "Stop here," I said.

"Why?"

"The plane is right over there." I pointed to the right. We could see very little in the dark.

"No, there's nothing over there but a terrace." He knew the area well.

"Let me go see."

"I'll go. You stay here," George said. His words were meant to comfort and his actions to protect me.

"I've come this far and I'm going all the way." I was stubbornly reaching for the door handle.

George gave a sigh and a slight nod of his head. "Come on then. Get out on my side."

He got out of the car. I slid across the driver's seat. He took my hand as if to let me know I would not face disaster alone. We waded through a ditch filled knee-deep with snow.

We could see contrast between bare ground and snow spots as we crossed a small part of the field and stopped at the terrace. After one glance, George waved the boy following us back to the car. He must have said something, but I was oblivious to everything except the plane wreckage, the fuselage partially intact, the rest of the plane scattered in many pieces. Nearby a body was lying on the ground.

"Here's one," George said, as he walked toward the form.

I stopped near the fuselage as he walked forward. "Is he large or small?" I questioned.

"Small," he said.

In a dazed voice I replied, "Then he's mine." My mind refused to accept that as fact, however, so I asked what kind of jacket he had on. "Is it a wool jacket or a slick finish?" Burl had on a nylon flight jacket and Charlie had on brown wool, I remembered.

George leaned over. "A slick finish—"

"Then he isn't mine." The voice I used sounded distant to me.

I walked closer to the largest piece of wreckage and felt around in the darkness under it. Charlie's body was still strapped in, upside down. This area seemed darker than that surrounding us.

"He's in here." I pulled down and out on his shirt tail and felt his skin. I thought he felt warm.

I seemed to be two people—one knelt, feeling the seat belt, clothing, and body of my loved one. The other was behind me watching actions of someone who seemed remote in feeling. It was a strange sensation. I felt that Charlie was watching me, too. He seemed to be above, but very close, while I touched his body below. It was as if we each had two forms. One was physical below, and one of some other form above and behind—watching, understanding, but not judging.

"He's still warm," I called to George as he walked back toward me.

George felt Charlie's body. "No. He's dead." His voice projected both surrender and sorrow.

"You can't be sure," I protested.

"Yes, I'm sure."

The demolished plane parts underlined what I wanted to cross out.

"Are you positive?"

"Yes, I'm positive."

My recent certainty split. Two forces began battle within me. "It's over. You can go now. He's dead," a voice in my head stated flatly.

But my feet refused to move, for my heart violently disagreed. "No! No! I refuse to accept it. It can't be true!"

III

George took my hand once more, and we walked back toward the road. It was bitter cold. I felt empty. By the time we recrossed the ditch, two or three cars with flashing red lights had arrived. The images of those lights are branded forever in my mind.

When we returned to the front seat of the car I submitted to one moment of hysteria. I can still hear the deep sobs in my mind. I wouldn't ever have planned finding Charlie that way, but I was compelled to go.

Looking back, I believe God led me to the crash site. I had always been expert at thinking problems would go away if I ignored them. I know now that they have to be accepted, discussed, and worked on to improve.

Charlie's death was going to be hard for me to accept but it was a reality.

We went back into town and the doctor came to the parsonage again, this time with a sedative for me. My mind functioned well long enough for me to telephone relatives and the doctor back home, then relaxed some, although sedation worked very little, for I slept only thirty minutes. I rested before and after that but I felt as if I were floating in the air above the bed, not really supported by anything.

Charlie and I had discussed funeral services once—not at length, for I feared such talk. I preferred to ignore the fact that we age and die, hoping I wouldn't age and never believing he could die early. Charlie believed in a memorial service; in not viewing the body. Recalling his wishes, I decided we would have a closed casket ceremony. Besides, I wanted my children to remember their daddy with his laughing good looks, alive and well.

A ground blizzard came before dawn. The cold wind scattered diapers and little blankets across the field near the plane. I can still picture Don's wife bringing in toys and washing them in the kitchen sink later in the morning. No one was allowed to touch anything else around the crash site for hours. The cold snow outside was a counterpart for the numbness in my heart.

Ruthy woke up at 11:00 A.M. Her eyes wouldn't focus for a while. "Hi, Aunt Joan," she said as my sister arrived from Omaha. "What happened?" I don't recall who told her about the airplane or her daddy, although she told me later that I did it. I do remember my sister brought me a black dress to replace my gay red one.

At home our children were told of the accident as they awakened.

Around noon Joan, Ruth, and I walked next door to the church. I sat down at the piano and played a couple of hymns from memory. Then I played from the music book, "God Will Take Care of You," and began to sing. Charlie's voice joined in just like past vocal duets.

He seemed near to me, tuning his tenor voice to match my alto. I didn't want to stop singing or even breathe.

I caught a cupful of comfort from those few moments and dismissed all negative thoughts about how sensible it seemed. Could it be real? Ruthy said she heard it, too.

Charlie's body was not released until Monday evening. FAA investigators coming to seek the cause of the crash were delayed until Tuesday afternoon. I wanted to go on home. I couldn't wait any longer. I needed to get to my other three children.

Tuesday morning, my sister Joan and her husband drove us over icy roads back to Colorado Springs. I don't remember who put Charlie's body on an airplane or what we did as we retraced our steps and returned to the edge of the mountain, Colorado Springs.

When we arrived home after lunch our living room was filled with friends and relatives. Their chatter was like a cloudburst, then an avalanche of rushing water moving toward me, an irritating crescendo that would wash me off my feet. I wanted to shout, "Go away! Get out!" and then retreat to the quiet of my bedroom, and if necessary, hide under the bed.

Choosing a casket, talking to ministers, accepting food I couldn't eat, visiting, and trying to remember well-known names filled me with confusion.

We had a private funeral service and burial with relatives in attendance Thursday morning. Quiet, but not peaceful.

We had protected our children overmuch in the past. The boys had never been to a funeral; the girls had attended one unexpectedly while visiting friends, but even that was not due to any wisdom of ours. Charlie and I had discussed taking them to one earlier, but postponed it.

Lack of communication was soon evident. "Where is my daddy's body buried?" David asked as we left the casket at the cemetery. In our attempt to tell him of his father's soul, we hadn't made ourselves clear about the physical body.

We had a public memorial service Thursday night at which we used resurrection music. This is rare even for Christians who should value it especially at such a time.

"It was new to see hope and joy, rather than tears and sadness," a girl friend commented afterwards. My emotions were as lifeless as spring flowers during the deadliest winter, but fragments of sentences from the children began to penetrate my consciousness.

"I wish I had died with Daddy in that plane crash," Ruthy vocalized dramatically. There were times when I almost agreed with her.

I knew we needed assurance. I wasn't certain who was going to answer questions for me so that I could properly comfort the children. Many of us don't face thoughts of death squarely. Our society helps very little with sensible adjustments because it encourages us to neglect preparing ourselves at all.

Relatives and friends showed their love constantly. They talked to the children, looked after our needs, and took care of a million details. Kathy Odum came and stayed a week. She was a special friend who had helped me earlier and would strengthen me in the months ahead. She took charge of everything, including unmarked dishes, a list of people who needed to be thanked for food, origin of flowers delivered to the house, and telephone calls.

I walked in a fog, reacted without thinking, and lived in a mechanical world. I couldn't really believe Charlie was dead. My head and heart were still arguing about whether to accept or reject the truth. Foolishly, I thought it best to deny my tears, thinking they might hinder the children's adjustment.

Sometimes I would allow myself to be fooled for a split second. I'd search the face of every driver of a maroon Volkswagen, looking for my husband. Always, I'd have to accept the disappointing moment of reality —it *wasn't* Charlie.

One evening Joan and I were sitting on my bed talking and folding clean clothes. I heard footsteps coming down the hall and my heart began a speedy thumping. Then reality grew into a lump in my throat that I could hardly speak through.

"I have just realized that I will *never* hear Charlie's footsteps coming down the hall again," I said.

But I found memories to remind me of him everywhere.

IV

Throughout January, an involuntary shiver frequently took possession of my body. Over and over I repeated, "God will take care of us." It was natural for that comment to surface from beneath the shock because I had attended Sunday School and church all my life. I believed it, but I was unable to prevent complete desolation from consuming me at times. Days were lonely, even when several people surrounded me. There wasn't one thing to look forward to, so I tried to prevent thoughts of the future. It didn't help much to think of the past either, for the purpose of those years seemed to elude me.

Never had I ever pictured so much trouble in my life. In my daydreams I built castles, not dungeons. My mind was filled with pleasant things—laughter, love, heroes—and if I ever imagined anything bad, I made myself the heroine. In reality, my castle walls disintegrated and I lived in a dark hole. It took all of my strength just to maintain a simple sense of emotional balance. Courage was missing, and I felt drained of energy.

The dental equipment at the office was as useless to me as a plane without a pilot. The weekend after the funeral it seemed necessary to take inventory so we could advertise for selling. An interested buyer during winter? New graduates or men who were coming out of the service wouldn't be taking the state exam for Colorado certification until June, six months in the future. Maybe someone interested would attend the area dental convention in Denver the following week. We should hurry. Two of Charlie's classmates, practicing dentistry in Colorado, gave freely of their time and knowledge to help inventory the office, but we didn't receive a serious inquiry for months.

Ten days later, I returned to my third-grade classroom. Portia, a student teacher whom I had requested, but hadn't met, preceded me. She was acquainted with the situation and children by the time I returned. She was efficient, understanding, and filled with workable ideas. I might have called her a blessing heaven-sent, but I wouldn't have realized the truth of my statement until later.

Having taught ten years, much of what I did was no longer complicated. If teaching at that time had required much clear, creative thinking, I probably would have failed the children completely.

Portia had the ability to take control quickly in many subject areas. I rationalized that the class didn't suffer too much from my incomplete presence. Teaching was good mental and physical therapy.

I was expected, needed, and felt secure at school. My principal had lost his wife a few months earlier, so he was able to identify with my feelings. I appreciated the uncomplaining parents of those days.

Mr. and Mrs. Christian Layman (friends who prefer to remain anonymous) gave Kathy and Ruthy loving attention during two of our worst days. I recalled when we had met the Laymans, nine months prior to Charlie's death. Mr. Layman had come to speak at our Christian Business and Professional Women's dinner meeting.

He radiated confidence, had a warm accepting personality, and was not afraid to share his innermost thoughts with us. He told us of his early life, how Billy Graham helped him to accept the Lord Jesus Christ, and what God had done since to help make him a successful businessman.

I wanted to hear more about the joy he felt and hoped he would share his experience with Charlie, too. After the meeting I approached him and his wife at the head table.

"I'd like my husband to meet you. Would you come to our house for dessert some evening?" It seemed so important to me that I could hardly wait for their answer.

"We will come if it is all right with your husband, but we don't go anywhere unwanted," Mrs. Layman answered.

I drove home elated. "I met some people tonight and I'd like you to meet them, too. Could they come over for dessert this Friday evening?" I asked Charlie.

"Yes, if it's important to you."

We thought a certain front necessary to success, so we weren't eager to have strangers visit us. Our furniture and appliances were about to fall apart. Charlie had changed careers, and was one of the older men among the students while attending dental school, his second time through college. He had been struggling hard to build a dental practice. Many nights he would return to the office and do his own laboratory work to save expense and to get things done in a way he could accept.

That Friday evening we had a pleasant visit. Mr. Layman invited Charlie to the YMCA the following week for a game of handball. A friendship between them developed slowly and I was pleased. But time was cut short for that friendship.

When Mr. Layman came to see me after Charlie's funeral, he was the first person who had offered to read a scripture and pray with me. From his visit, I absorbed a measure of peace. When he read Deuteronomy 33:27—"The eternal God is thy refuge, and underneath are the everlasting arms"—and told me that I could *rest* securely in those arms, I knew at once the meaning of words heard many times without total understanding. It was as if the Lord were assuring me that he really would help me. Without those arms holding me, I would have felt that I was falling through black space forever. Into my valley of the shadow of death came the first bit of true light from eternity.

Mr. Layman said a week or so later, "I've had some experience in insurance. Could I help you by filling out the necessary forms?" I willingly accepted his help.

He finally assumed the task of caring for all the paper work involved with social security and the veteran's administration. He helped with estate business and taught me about investing insurance proceeds. It wasn't a small job, and I was grateful.

Charlie had warned me in December that he refused to borrow again to pay life insurance premiums, as he had been doing through dental school. I didn't believe he was serious but I was mistaken. We were well into the thirty day grace period on two different policies when he died. Mutual of New York never once questioned the timing and paid us immediately. Charlie's death also legally cancelled the need to repay our schooling loan from the government.

Thinking back later I realized that God had definitely been taking care of us. Charlie had changed professions, borrowed money, and skimped to make certain there would be adequate college financing for our children. We were assured of that in spite of our recent circumstances of debt as the first month of the new year came to a close, but I would rather have had Charlie alive than any amount of money to spend.

V

I stepped on the school nurse's scale in February. My weight had dropped from 128 to 103. It was nice, being a size 9, but my face looked as bare as an aspen tree without leaves. My appetite was as low as the sap in those trees, and since Charlie's death I couldn't even brush my teeth.

Every time I thought of teeth I remembered Charlie working on mine. I finally appealed to the dentist friend who was completing Charlie's unfinished work. Walking into his office made my knees shake for I associated Charlie with that particular building, as well as with any dentist.

"Ron, I've got a problem," I managed to mumble.

"What's the trouble?" His voice and manner were gentle.

"Each morning I struggle to eat, and then try to brush my teeth so I can go to school. As soon as I stick my brush in my mouth my breakfast comes up. Would you clean my teeth?"

"Come and sit in my chair and let me have a look." He led the way into an operatory.

"I can't stand it. My teeth feel terrible. If this keeps up, they'll all fall out."

"Mary, relax. Let me clean them for you." He put a bib around my neck. "If you continue to have this problem, I'll clean them for you often—until you get over it." He treated me as carefully as he would a two-year-old. Memories of Charlie in his blue and white striped dental gown overpowered me and I began to tremble. Ron offered to finish at another time.

"I've got to learn to sit in a dentist's chair again. It might as well be now. I'm sorry. Please go ahead."

"Rinse," he soon said.

A fresh, clean sensation and the smooth texture on the surface of my teeth told my tongue it was home free.

"It's amazing how differently our experiences make us react individually," I said after I rinsed out my mouth.

"I don't think your reaction is unexpected," Ron said and then led me into his conference office. "How are the children?"

"Paul David, the youngest, doesn't seem to be fully aware of all the circumstances. He does better than the rest of us about living one day at a time. He is busy thinking of football heroes. He seems to feel unworthy of wearing good clothes. He tears the pockets right off new blue jeans." I glanced along the shelves at familiar dental books.

"How is Ruthy?"

"She says things unintentionally that cut into my heart like a knife. She verbalizes, but still—that is better than keeping it inside. She remains toothpick thin and is usually chewing a fingernail. She has invented and organized a '*Charlie Club*' and wants her friends to join. She is the only one of us who seems able to talk about him at all." I gazed at certificates on the office wall while Ron talked to a patient on the telephone for a moment.

"Are the older two doing okay?"

"Kathy doesn't say much. She spends time on her studies and is dependable. She saves me lots of steps and puts dinner on if I'm late from school. She is withdrawn and has gone back into the world of shyness she nearly outgrew."

Ron's assistant came to the door. He waved her away.

"Danny is covering up his feelings, too. Involved in school activities. Learning to ski. I am surprised at how well he does. I watched him ski at the Broadmoor one night. It scared me." I stood and started toward the door, for I knew the value of his time.

"How is school?"

"Fine. I have a capable student teacher."

"Are you still living in the same house you shared with Charlie?"

"Yes."

"Call me when you need me."

"Thanks a million, Ron."

He understood the trauma involved in my visit. I had been concerned for my children and their emotions, but I was the one who had the most trouble staying calm when suddenly faced with memories. When the children went to the dentist later, their attempts at self-control surpassed mine. Ron even had Ruthy assisting him!

VI

By the beginning of March, two months after Charlie's death, I developed a small sense of humor and started numbering my strange moods, deep depressions, and rare moments of feeling adaptable.

Any small change in my plans or situation would make me fear all of my foundations, for the future might fall apart again. Sometimes a spurt of energy would push me toward believing I could cope with four children alone. At other times, my spirit would plummet like the mercury in a thermometer lying on a winter mountainside.

A paralyzing depression was most apt to grip me near bedtime. Taking even one step then demanded sturdy crutches of courage. Some of my dreams were as paralyzing as finding the plane crash.

I learned to joke a little. I'm in "phase thirteen," later "phase nineteen," and months later, "phase one hundred and five." Dozens of numbers were skipped, but it didn't matter. Emotional changes and stages went on indefinitely. Reading a small book, *Good Grief,* which explained reactions to death, helped me accept myself as normal. I wish I could have read it earlier.

Charlie and I had purchased a used car in December and no one could find the old title. Charlie's check to the state office for a new title had been returned when our bank account was temporarily frozen by law at his death. We searched through every drawer, book, and box.

Sally, Charlie's dental assistant, gave generously of her time to help me. She came over to the house one evening and we sat at the kitchen table reviewing patient records. We discussed the car title, too.

"I've looked through everything and I can't find it," she said.

"What shall we do with these old printed office checks with Charlie's name on them?" When I was in doubt regarding office matters, I asked Sally. She had a marvelous memory concerning the total office situation, the work done in the past on patients, and how to take care of business details.

"Since we have the new estate checks we might as well tear them up." Sally picked up the checkbook to destroy the old checks, and there was the car title— tucked under the last page.

I pulled the calendar off the wall and quickly carried it over to the table. "Look, Sally!" There in the square for that very date my brother-in-law had written, "If no car title by today, begin the procedure to get a new one through the state department. Don't wait any longer." Some work seemed to be taking care of itself, I thought at the time. I began to list in my mind odd little incidents that occurred which made life easier for me. How could they all be just coincidence?

"Sally, have you received any more payments on accounts?"

"Mary, it's discouraging. I know how perfectly Charlie completed his work. You wouldn't believe the number of fillings that are falling out, now that he isn't here to check on them." We tried to laugh about it. Patients invented all types of excuses to prevent paying money my husband had rightfully earned.

A letter came from an experienced dentist in Texas who wanted to move to Colorado Springs. We didn't have to wait until June and were pleased to be able to sell the dental equipment.

During March and April there seemed to be a contest developing between my self-control and other, more natural emotions. I wanted to face the feelings connected with all the places Charlie and I had been together. I thought I would visit each place quickly and get it over with, assuming incorrectly that such feelings wouldn't return.

I even forced myself to continue to sing in the choir. When we began practicing the Easter music about death, doubt punctured my serenity. My nerves shouted "Blast Off!" and I thought they would thrust me straight up through the roof before I could get past the piano and out of the room. I admitted defeat.

"Help! Help!" That was all I could spit out when I found my hands steady enough to drive to a girl friend's home and knock on her door. Gerie had been a widow for a year and was very understanding. She always helped me accept myself and my fluctuating moods, assuring me I was normal.

"What's your problem, doll?" Her tall figure and calm movements comforted me as she invited me inside.

"I just left choir practice—right in the middle!"

"So? Sit down and have a cup of tea." She efficiently placed a pan of water on the stove burner.

"I don't think I can go back, ever." A large sigh drained my last remaining bit of strength.

"Well, maybe you're pushing yourself too hard. Why don't you slow down and face things when you have to, one at a time, instead of trying to prove to yourself that you can do it all this minute?"

Her advice seemed wise. It sounded a little like a comment I had heard a couple of times when business details threatened to suffocate me. "You don't have to make that decision *today*."

I tried to return to that choir and that church several times, but I was never comfortable there where memories of Charlie kept me from thinking of anything else.

During the last of April I began to realize that wherever I went there were memories of myself as part of a couple. Our society convinced me I was out of place. I wasn't part of anything except a broken family. This weird feeling led to further depression.

Late Friday afternoon, just before Mother's Day, Dan drove us through the sunny countryside to Denver where we planned to spend the weekend. As we traveled along the highway, stately green trees echoed the fresh beauty of mountain springtime which should have thawed my heart, but it was still frozen in a block of shock.

"I'd like to read to you as we ride," I told my children. "I have a book here about a widow and her family. I think some of her problems are like some of ours. If it upsets you, just say so, and I'll quit."

No one answered, so I picked up the book from my lap and began to read aloud. Two chapters later, tears four months overdue flooded my face. With trembling hands, I closed the book.

"If *who* gets upset?" teased Ruthy, leaning over from the back seat of the car to see my face.

The weight of the total pressure of grief finally forced my desert-dry eyes into being channels for a personal cloudburst. I couldn't stop crying for three days.

"It's not fair to be upset on Mother's Day when it's the father of the family we've lost," I sobbed on Sunday. My feelings were twisted and stretched as tight as the rubber band on Dave's toy airplane. Tense. Prepared for flight.

Returning home Sunday evening the children were pleasantly planning their summer. I was able to share their relief about school ending soon. Even though I enjoyed being an active primary teacher, I was ready to trade my rushed schedule for a vacation.

Passing the Air Force Academy area at dusk, we noticed a small airplane approaching the landing strip near the highway. The flashing lights settled closer to the horizon. I gasped. Memories from New Year's Day frosted my mind again.

I turned over and over trying to go to sleep that night, and when I finally slept I dreamed I found Charlie on a mountainside, unable to speak.

It seemed unfair for me to have to write "deceased" regarding *father* on the children's school papers. Worse yet, my pride as a dentist's wife was shattered.

Technically, I didn't even belong in that field of interest anymore, yet I was continually accepted by Charlie's classmates. We enjoyed a spring picnic with them and their families. I think the wives may have wondered why I preferred to be with the men talking, but no one said a word about it. Dental discussions were oddly comforting.

Sometimes I felt I had worked hard and scrimped many years so Charlie could advance all for nothing. Then I remembered his pride in the title of "Dr." during the last two and a half years of his life and was glad I had been able to help him obtain a measure of success.

Holidays and anniversaries were full of memories. I never knew when I'd have a relapse into mild shock. Anticipated hurt could sometimes be lessened by a tranquilizer taken in advance. If I allowed myself to talk about the plane crash I knew that I would need a sleeping pill that night.

A song could turn back all of the present calendar, and I would relive some other day. I couldn't sing "Dear Heart, Wish You Were Here," and ever get all the way through. I did spend hours playing the piano which released some of my tension.

The numbness began to leave after I cried that whole weekend early in May. I began to feel emotions and let myself remember more. There were times when I would have stayed in shock had I been given a choice.

The children were alone many evenings. They actually lost both parents for a while. I was there, but only physically. It was as if I were taking two muscle relaxants every three hours. I could move easily but not really think or react properly.

Other times, when I could have been home, at least physically, I wasn't—for I could not sit down at the end of a school day and concentrate or relax in that house. Every evening began the same—Good intentions of staying home with the children. After being quiet for about five minutes, I could think of at least three places more lively and less filled with memories.

Before Charlie died I rested or escaped by reading. Now I found it hard to complete even one short story, not only hard, but really impossible.

Since I couldn't concentrate well enough to follow the plot, movies weren't satisfying. Bars weren't for me because I was unfamiliar with them, felt unsafe there, and besides I didn't like liquor, although in my search for something to occupy myself I tried a few times.

That left roller skating with the children—which was filled with memories of Charlie—or spending time with friends.

Kathy Odum always welcomed me with a hot cup of tea and some delicious calorie-laden dessert made in her kitchen. She had been widowed twice but still had ample energy and was not above doing my mending!

Gerie, too, welcomed me with two good listening ears and a benevolent attitude. She developed a genuine affinity for my children which they returned.

I began to realize how God uses people to transmit His love.

Part II

... I will fear no evil; for
Thou art with me ...

VII

Before Memorial Day the children and I put some flowers on Charlie's grave.

"We'll need to come back another evening so I can clip the grass around the headstone," Danny said.

"Could we get a great big stone for daddy's grave?" Kathy asked.

"No, I think the one the government furnished because he was in the Air Force is adequate. It doesn't really matter that much does it?" I thought I had explained the lack of a large stone acceptably, but the question kept returning.

"I don't know," she answered.

"The money we have can be more wisely spent on your college education," I replied.

I couldn't help driving out to the cemetery now and then, but I resolved not to be a daily grave watcher, as a cousin of mine had been for months after her husband died, for I didn't believe that the part of Charlie I loved was locked underground. I thought there were better ways to spend my time.

Mr. and Mrs. Layman invited me to go with them to hear three interesting speakers. We went first to the home of some of their friends. A pleasant hostess greeted us at the door and directed us to steps that led to the basement.

"What a radiant face she has," I said, as we walked down. My mind was filled with wonder for she seemed to know some important secret.

We sat on folding chairs, fifty or more people, as we crowded into a small area to hear the teacher. He had spent time studying the Bible for longer than I had lived and was positive about what he believed. I asked many questions, realized I was privileged to be there, and sometimes felt stupid because I didn't know as much as some of the teen-agers about the Scripture.

John believed God's promises. He made them sound clear and wonderful. He had living proof of answer to prayer.

"For many years my wife and I have been the house-parents of a children's home. We never solicit funds, furniture, clothing, or food. People have helped us because they recognize our need," he said in answer to my question about his profession.

God *is* faithful, some inner voice whispered to me.

Together we read from Matthew 6:33, "But seek ye first the kingdom of God, and his righteousness; and all these things shall be added unto you." That had actually happened to John. I knew that Scripture, but this was the first time it had meaning for me. His example from real life was something I could understand.

Would it work for me?

Bible study became very important. God's promises were so magnetic! I began to think about them part of the time instead of my unhappy situation as a widow.

School duties continued for a few more days. Watching a robin fly across the playground one morning I saw expanding clouds climbing over Pike's Peak. Nearly every day the peak would be clear as I went to school, but by recess clouds were forming and moving in. As I kept looking that time, they gradually covered the mountaintop, hiding it from view. I couldn't see it, but I knew it was there, for I could see it again each new morning.

I repeated Isaiah 54:10 to myself, a verse from our Bible study of the night before. It said, "For the mountains shall depart, and the hills be removed; but my kindness shall not depart from thee, neither shall the covenant of my peace be removed, saith the Lord, that hath mercy on thee." So I reasoned that God was with me, even if I couldn't see Him during the times when sorrow seemed to hide Him from me.

God moved a little closer to me in my mind than He had been—a little way down from the faraway heavens, off the large white cloud where He had seemed to live since I was three.

Next, the Laymans suggested a visit to a different Sunday school class, in a church not my own.

"I don't belong there." I reminded them. "What will the members say? And what will my friends and relatives think when they find out?"

"Just visit a few times," they gently insisted.

I found it hard not to feel sneaky as I slipped in and out of a strange church during the Sunday School hour, yet I seemed to absorb strength from every lesson. Each Sunday something was said, even if it was in the closing prayer, that seemed to be meant to comfort me. I gained courage and learned more about how God loved and cared for me. I began to desire more knowledge of God and to read the Bible for myself.

The teacher there drew for us a mental picture of Jesus and the disciples in the daily life they shared. In my mind, I could see the scenes he described.

He told us of Peter jumping over the side of a boat and walking toward Jesus on the water. I could imagine it so clearly that I could see drops of water splashing from his feet.

I turned to Peter's short prayer in Matthew 14:30, "Lord, save me," said in a moment of doubt and fear. I thought prayers had to be lengthy to be valid, but Peter said only three words and Christ Jesus responded immediately.

Then Bob prayed as if God were right there with us, saying "You" instead of "Thee" and "Thou," and talking to God in a conversational way. It was different than anything I had ever heard, and it was astounding to me. I began to suspect that some people knew God in some special way, that He is approachable, and that human beings could be on very friendly terms with Him.

Discussing experiences with the Laymans later led to feelings that made my blood pressure pound. They seemed so certain about possessing eternal life that I became angry. I lived within my personalized belief that I must work my way to heaven, that I'd best die on a day I had been careful to ask forgiveness, and that I wouldn't know if I'd actually earned a pleasant eternity until I died.

"How can you be so *sure* that you know?" I questioned, realizing for the first time what foolish, frustrated, not-knowing living I'd been through, and hoping that they did know and would tell me. I thought maybe

I had been sure once, but over the years I had grown very uncertain.

"The Bible tells us." Mrs. Layman was very patient with me. She spoke confidently as from Romans 3:23 she quoted, "For all have sinned, and come short of the glory of God."

I knew my life wasn't free of sin and admitted it.

Then from Romans 6:23, "For the wages of sin is death; but the gift of God is eternal life through Jesus Christ our Lord."

"I never did notice the word *gift* standing out so clearly. I thought you went to heaven by the way you lived, doing everything as right as you could," I said.

"Do you believe in the Bible?"

"Yes."

"Every verse?"

"Yes."

"We, too, believe in every verse of the Bible, and we like Ephesians 2:8 and 9," she answered.

We searched the pages and found, "For by grace are ye saved through faith; and that not of yourselves: it is the gift of God: Not of works, lest any man should boast."

"What does *grace* mean?" was my next question.

"An easy way to explain it is 'unmerited favor.' "

"I never heard that before."

Mrs. Layman continued, "If you want to *know* you have eternal life, all you need to do is ask forgiveness for your sins. Then, if you ask, believing, and will receive Him, He will come to live inside you in the form of the Holy Spirit. Then you'll know. From inside, He will help you accept what has happened in your life, be with you all the time, and also help you understand the Scriptures."

"I accepted Christ when I was eleven years old, but I think it was just as my Savior, for I never really let Him take over as Lord of my life. I had some plans of my own that always came first, like marrying Charlie. My parents have always—"

"This is a personal relationship between you and God. It has nothing to do with your parents. You see, God doesn't have any grandchildren. You are either His child or you're not."

It sounded simple and desirable. I wanted to try it. But there was a small stubborn part of me that couldn't give in right at that moment.

The third place I went with the Laymans was a small church that had services on Sunday nights, as well as Sunday mornings, which was unusual to me. Speaking of my reaction that first Sunday evening one of my friends said later, "You lit up like a light bulb." I *was* beginning to feel lighter inside.

"All the songs were inspirational and everybody sang," I began telling other teachers on Monday about the Sunday night service. "They are hymns I have known for years, but haven't heard for a long time." I couldn't keep still.

"An added bonus was evident when the pastor began to teach," I told my children. "He gave us background for each chapter, skipped nothing, and clearly explained each verse." They would have to go and see.

Soon I could smile about the half-starved way I gobbled Scriptural teaching. It was like the beauty and excitement of mountain scenery. I couldn't possibly get enough.

It took only one week for me to break an unwritten rule that was nevertheless stamped in my brain, *DON'T MARK IN YOUR BIBLE.* I began to write comments and explanations in all the margins as I listened and learned.

In the weeks that followed, I felt like a sponge that had been dried out for years. To become pliable and usable, I required rain. God's word was my moisture. Truly, it was the water of life! I could feel myself coming alive again. I took notes as if it were a life or death matter, and it was—eternal life!!

New Christian friends cared for me because God loved me and I learned to love them because they were His. Their love of God helped expand mine. Sleepy emotions began to awaken and come up out of the foggy valley of my mind, and I began to view life from a higher plain at times. But not steadily yet. It was as if I had to climb up and down many foothills before I would have a view from the top of the valley.

June fourth came. It was my seventeenth wedding anniversary date—my first as a widow. I felt lost, as if I were part of a vanished dream, but I overcame my natural inclination to live in the past and consciously returned to thoughts of travel planned for this month and the possibility of moving to a larger home.

I asked the Laymans if they would help me find a house. We drove around in the area I wanted to see. We didn't find anything.

"You go on your trip and have a good time. If the Lord wants you to move, there will be a house ready to rent when you return." They believed that would really happen.

VIII

Remembering our plans for early summer cheered me. My sister and her husband had offered to share a trip to New York City and Washington, D.C. The children could profit educationally from the trip. Also, it was something to look forward to—a *must* for widows. My brother-in-law accepted an offer from a friend and borrowed his station wagon.

When we arrived in New York, we went to the top of the Empire State Building, rode a boat under numerous bridges around Manhattan Island, and were glad we didn't need to ride the noisy subway regularly.

Riding across town in the back of the station wagon, I woke up from a nap in time to see the Federal Aviation Association building down a side street. Why hadn't I stayed asleep a bit longer? Memories stirred. I had recently received a letter from that office building stating that the probable cause of Charlie's plane crash was vertigo, a loss of equilibrium.

When we drove into Washington, my throat contracted. This was a place Charlie and I had planned to see together but here we were without him. I cried again. It just didn't seem fair.

I recalled high school history and English classes that my father and mother had taught as I stood in Lincoln's Memorial. It was my favorite spot on our sightseeing trip. I took an individual picture of each child standing in front of Mr. Lincoln.

At the Washington Monument we had to sit in benches around the tall spire as we waited in line.

"We are going to race you to the top," a couple of the children decided.

"Up all those steps?" I asked.

"We won," the thrilled voices of the two children who walked up met those of us who rode to the top. I found myself wishing for some of their energy.

Ruthy became lost inside the United States Capitol building. I immediately pictured another funeral and the loss of my children one by one. My sister stood still and held my hand so I wouldn't panic. My knees were too weak to walk. My brother-in-law and Danny searched.

A guard soon found her standing at the bottom of the last flight of steps we had climbed. I trembled inside for thirty minutes.

We rested in a cabin in the Pocono Mountains with relatives and were reminded of our Colorado home as blue skies, cotton puff clouds, and tree soldiers were reflected in the lake nearby.

My only desire to hurry home occurred when we passed a terrible accident on the Pennsylvania Turnpike. My nerve endings waved at my skin for a release. Memory of the plane wreckage and Charlie's body zoomed to my consciousness in a jet stream. It was helpful to be with understanding family members, as the tears again exposed and eased my inner turmoil.

"I'm upset because my minister didn't read the Scriptures and pray with me when Charlie died," I complained bitterly to my sister. We were sitting on the edge of a motel pool watching the children swim. We had begun our journey back toward home.

"What they say and do is left entirely up to them. They have some training in counseling, but they don't learn everything there is to know about it."

"Surely they should comfort a widow?"

"Different widows, or even people who are ill, have various ideas about what is comforting to them, personally. About the only way a minister can know what the widow would like is for her to tell him."

She should know. She's married to a minister, I thought.

"I guess he can't read minds," I grudgingly admitted. "Still, since eternal life is the only thing I can think of to look forward to pleasurably, I'd think he would at least have mentioned it when we were talking . . . I guess I'm in that bitter stage that is supposed to be normal!"

Life seemed to promise some restful moments as we headed for home with time to spare before a school routine forced us back to a more rigid schedule.

I thought of our need for more space and what the Laymans had said about finding a house. The children had been sleeping in two sets of bunkbeds. Danny was getting too tall to wiggle into and sleep comfortably there. Would I find a house?

I wondered. Would God bother with that?

In order for the Laymans to expect God to do anything like helping a person find a house, they must have had a lot of practice turning things over to Him with plenty of faith backing it up, I thought, as I began to look for one.

But the Laymans knew what they were doing, I decided, as I drove through a neighborhood moments later and saw a "FOR RENT" sign in the window of a three bedroom, split-level house. I went to the door.

"We'll be ready to move out in about a month," a lady told me. It was the right area and the rental cost was not out of line.

"It will be for sale in a year, with the rent applying to the final price if you want it for a permanent residence," she continued.

What a staggering surprise! I could hardly accept such information after only thirty minutes of searching. But I didn't let the opportunity pass.

Words to "His Eye Is on the Sparrow and I Know He Watches Me" went winging through my soul as I drove home to tell the children. I must consciously begin to leave out of my vocabulary such words as *fate* and *fortune,* I decided.

IX

My language wasn't the only thing that needed changing. I had accepted Charlie's yardstick and measured much of my life with it. Now I realized that using my own measuring tape was no better.

I was restless. What had been missing all along? I began to wonder if God had a gauge that I hadn't recognized or fully understood, one that would be more satisfying to me.

Moods flew high, nose-dived, and balanced erratically. I began to allow myself to feel more, but there was much that I refused to remember.

Topping each foothill, I was soon down in another low spot. Thinking of the task of rearing four children alone was too much, especially when I went to bed at night. Depression thrives in the dark, where burdens and fears grow beyond giant size.

My emotions were as explosive as the firecrackers popping in the neighborhood. My load grew enormous in size. I felt it was more than I could lift. How could already drooping shoulders carry added weight?

I didn't know who would help me solve my greatest problems in any permanent way, although many friends and relatives had offered help. What I required was mental, physical, and spiritual help. I longed to escape —to go to sleep and never wake up. Every part of me was saturated with weariness.

I telephoned Mr. and Mrs. Layman, getting them out of bed.

"Please come over. I feel like committing suicide and I'm the only parent these children have—and I know it's not right and it can't be but—"

They came at eleven. Having company forced me to pretend to be calm. We had another long discussion about God. I wanted to know more about the way they lived.

"How do you turn your life over to God?" I asked.

"We love Him, study His Word, and pray. Then we wait for His guidance. We hope that He will use us to help others. We praise Him in advance for what He is going to do."

They gave me some small cards from the Navigators with Scripture verses on them. I memorized 1 Corinthians 10:13 right away for it spoke to my heart.

"There hath no temptation taken you but such as is common to man; but God is faithful, who will not [permit] you to be tempted above that ye are able; but will, with the temptation also make a way to escape, that ye may be able to bear it."

It appeared that talking to two of God's representatives was His answer and my escape route that night. People who allowed Him to love me through them helped many times.

Long after midnight, as they were leaving, I ex-

pressed my real fear. It concerned the future of the
children.

"I doubt if I can manage to rear them and have
them turn out decently at all, in this age of teen-agers
doing their own thing."

"Why don't you just turn them all over to the Lord
and let Him take care of them?" Mrs. Layman answered.

Why hadn't I thought of that? Maybe I'd learn to
think that way some day. I didn't see any discrepancy
in my thinking that although I could not yet completely
turn my future over to Him, it would be natural to rest
in Him concerning the care of my children. So I accepted the idea of depositing them into His hands,
prayerfully did it, and part of the heaviness vanished
from my heart.

Resting in God gradually grew natural in that area of
my life. I had been trying to do everything for the children myself, felt that I should, and planned to feel very
egotistical about it.

What had really frightened me was the possibility of
a child getting into serious trouble. If that happened I'd
have to blame myself completely also, and I knew I
wouldn't be able to bear such terrible guilt.

From then on, I fed, clothed, and tried to guide my
children, knowing that the Lord would be with them
when I couldn't be present.

I met more of His human helpers, as they befriended
my children. Danny, Kathy, Ruthy, and Paul David
went through emotional bad times, just as I did, and
we had some upsetting events, but I never again really
worried about the outcome. I *knew* God would take
care of them.

Personally, I was receiving each week at least three liberal cups of living water, God's Word.

I realized that I needed to give my life completely to Him, and since I wouldn't, remembering Matthew 7:7, "Ask, and it shall be given you; seek, and ye shall find; knock, and it shall be opened unto you," I prayed that God would give me more faith.

I was reluctant because I was afraid He wouldn't understand some of my needs, He, Who made me! I had built a fair-sized wall between Him and me in my mind over the years as I plodded in my own direction, blaming Him for trouble I had gotten myself into, and that wall wasn't going to tumble easily. I think I expected Him to knock it down even though I had built it. I wasn't able to demolish it myself yet or certain that I really wanted it torn down.

I kept thinking I would have to give something up— freedom lost. I wanted God's help but was not willing to accept His total guidance. It was the only untried answer to my restlessness for as soon as I moved into our new house, I would have all that Charlie and I had dreamed of in the way of material things.

X

August heat surrounded us as we moved.

"Let us have the big bedroom with the separate bathroom," the girls said. "We'll share."

So the boys were given separate rooms for the first time in their lives. I took the den in our finished basement. Different surroundings helped us forget old feelings. It was fun choosing and buying new furniture.

As often as time, energy, and weather permitted, the children and I drove up into the mountains. I went alone many times, too. God seemed to speak peace to me through the natural beauty He has created.

The rocks seemed to say for Him, "I have been here for at least 1.7 billion years. I will last and My strength is great."

The stream seemed to bubble His wishes for my life, "Keep clean and pure and be happy. This makes you beautiful."

The pleasant breeze seemed to whisper through the aspen leaves, "I am here. Listen! Even if you can't see Me, I am close to you."

The pattern of growing things nearer the ground said of Him, "I have a plan and a purpose for the things I made. They are all intricate and lovely. Spring returns in nature. Spring will return for you and a new beginning will find its way into your life."

A feeling of renewal occurred several times during summer afternoons in the mountains. God's strength was there for me.

September arrived and I needed all of that strength. The school building was so full of memories when I returned that I found it hard to assemble my thoughts. I discovered a worn note in my school jacket that the office secretary had written many months ago. "Charlie telephoned that he will pick you up for lunch today."

I knew he wouldn't, ever again, and it upset me.

I couldn't get my bulletin boards covered. I usually put up colorful letters and pictures quickly and visited as I helped less experienced teachers, but I couldn't even think of one interesting idea to use in greeting my new class, and I had more than one bulletin board.

The second week, our principal learned that our enrollment was down from the expected number. One teacher would have to be transferred to another building. Fine! I moved into a more modern classroom closer to home. I believed God arranged that blessing, even though I hadn't thought to ask, so I said "Thank you, God" right out loud. Not many teachers knew me in that building which helped me to forget the past.

Danny's present actions were beginning to concern me enough that I couldn't forget them, however.

He had been very independent during his early years, so we had given him much responsibility and authority early. Even his playtime hadn't been as much as we would have liked. Because I had always been a mother who worked outside the home, the children learned to be capable in doing home chores. Being older, Danny and Kathy were given more responsibility, which sometimes included helping Ruthy and Paul David finish their work.

Now Danny was trying too hard to fill his father's shoes. He began to have trouble knowing where responsibility for his brother and sisters left off, and heavy-handedness began. I wished I had Charlie back to deal with it for me.

But the problem was mine, and I wasn't sure how to explain to Danny in a manner he would understand, without being overly critical. I loved him, but many of our discussions ended up in arguments. I was proud of his maturing mind, which began to equal mine in reasoning ability at times, and I didn't plan to push him out the door. Sometimes just the fact that he could remain calm and I would get emotional irritated me.

I couldn't ignore the problem because coming from school during late afternoons I was greeted at the door with such comments as: "Danny hit me." "Danny won't let me—" and so forth. Much resentment was building up from the three younger children.

I didn't stop to pray or even think about what I was going to say and Danny began to rebel when I talked to him. I grew hesitant about how to handle him.

"You won't ever paddle me again," he informed me. I accepted that as proper for this time in his life. So what else?

He had always accepted suggestions, if explanations were lengthy and understandable. My ability along those lines seemed to fail. I didn't want to take time to be a good diplomat.

Discussing it with one of the many new friends I came to know led to this idea:

"Why don't you follow your own school teaching advice and take away some of his privileges?"

I said, "He doesn't have any." I would have been upset if a parent had told me that.

"Well, he will be old enough to have a car of his own next February. Why don't you get a calendar and mark off one day for each time he oversteps his bounds? Discuss it with him, so he will be aware of what is happening. Include the times he hits one of the children or talks back to you. Let him do without the car when the time comes, one day for each day that you have crossed off."

I followed that advice, discussed it with Danny, and found him willing to accept the plan. He lost three days during the first week and then it tapered off. We saw so much change in his personality and actions during autumn that close relatives and friends began to comment, "I've noticed a change in Danny."

The girls invited friends in for sleepless slumber parties in front of the fireplace. When my father visited, he helped the boys fix up a Ping-Pong table. We sometimes had popcorn all over the basement. I half-heartedly complained about the confusion and secretly felt pleased that the children could express a portion of happiness. It was a mother language they understood.

Aspen leaves were turning gold before I could finally accept the fact and actually say out loud, "I am a widow."

I was determined to help others walk through dark valleys, for thinking of others was healthy. I visited and shared experiences with other widows.

"Let's go out to lunch," I frequently suggested to a

newer widow on a Saturday. Sometimes it upset me to try to cheer them. But when depression decided to come and stay for the winter it was unwelcome. Could I resist?

I had bothered the Laymans so much that I felt guilty just considering a telephone call to them. So I thought of what they would tell me to do about feeling unhappy.

"Count your blessings!" I could almost hear them say. That was no consolation earlier but it helped now. I also made certain that I didn't miss any Bible learning opportunities.

Concerned more with other essentials, I neglected to take care of my health. I caught a leveling case of the flu and was in bed several days. I was forced to slow down, to be alone, and think . . .

Flat on my back, I puzzled over the reason I kept resisting Christ. It was as if I peeked at him through a crack in a door, but wouldn't invite Him inside. Accepted, but not completely. Still, He persisted in His plan to have me for His own, waiting just outside the door of my heart like a gentleman, seeking, but not forcing admittance.

I acknowledged to myself that if I sincerely wanted to receive the Lord's help personally and without guilt, I would have to ask Him to take control of *my* life, not just ask Him to care for my children——not just profess to be a Christian, but practice being one. I struggled, for it meant putting Him first, above everything.

To totally put myself into His care was hard, for there were some things I kept thinking I knew best about, but I did surrender, and wrote in large letters on a little scrap of paper so it would be firmly impressed on my own mind—

"HIS, FINALLY!!!"

Many thoughts were in my mind that morning as bits and pieces I had learned about God throughout my lifetime finally fit together and made a colorful, completed picture.

This is a list I made for myself:

He loves me.

He has forgiven my sins.

He died for me and I've accepted His gift of eternal life.

He is right here with me.

He never ceases to help me.

His answers are available and much more helpful than anything I could figure out or make happen.

His ability to foresee and arrange surpasses mine.

He will clarify everything when I see Him. (Beautiful thought—seeing Him!)

Life with Him will make all of earth's troubles appear very small in retrospect.

I want to say "thank You" by doing things for Him.

I want to be used by Him.

I want my children and everyone to feel this secure freedom—in Him!

I love all of His children, even if they don't know they are His.

At that moment of conquering my selfishness and turning control over to the Lord to live within His will, complete peace filled an empty spot in my heart that was meant to hold only His love. The remainder of a weight I had always carried withdrew and I was free.

Immediately, I knew my own worth. The Lord valued my life and had a purpose for it that He would help me fulfill. (I didn't realize then the many plans He was already working on to provide happiness for me.) I decided that circumstances in my life on earth would never be allowed to defeat me again. I knew He would give me the strength to live by that decision.

The next week one of my friends told me that when I took sin out of my life I would have to put something good in, or the devil would take advantage of the space.

Talking of the devil, I put pictures of witches up on my bulletin board for school.

Then I began to read inspirational books. They were stories of what the Lord had done for others individually, told in open, personal fashion.

Those stories were used to fill up the place and time where depression had lived and grown. Strange, because I had felt uncomfortable when hearing the word *testimony* in any conversation during past years, and now I had added it to my vocabulary.

I also found some inspirational music. Religious recordings were really a soothing salve to my weary, learn-not-to-worry heart.

Amazed, I said to another widow, toward the end of October, "I have begun to look forward to the end of the day," and explained why.

"After the children are settled and I can go to bed, I put on a stack of records, words of comfort and love. 'It Will Be Worth It All' makes me picture Christ's face and my being with Him for all eternity as I drift off to sleep. My mind is blanketed with the truth of His love and care."

I thought of my new life goals. What were they, other than getting the children properly reared? What way could I repay Christ for the peace in my heart and for His death on the cross which guaranteed my eternal life?

I couldn't see to the end of the pathway, but at least He lent Light enough for a few steps at a time. Faith would pick me up if I faltered.

As I looked to Him for complete guidance now, I expected to begin seeing Him work more actively in the lives of my children.

XI

A ray of Christ's light was shining along my pathway the day Kathy Odum, in her usual thoughtful way, decided to help me encourage Danny to find a deeper meaning for living.

"Why don't you get acquainted with Young Life work and get him to attend their meetings?" she asked as I copied off a cranberry jello recipe for Thanksgiving.

"I can't handle one more thing. With four children, teaching, and church activities, I don't need one more thing." My conscience called me. Was I just being stubborn?

She kept suggesting and toward the end of November, I went to a meeting with her where slides were shown of Young Life activities, including their summer camps. The spiritual emphasis makes the organization worthwhile, an inner voice seemed to say to me, so I admitted to her that I felt agreeable to her suggestion.

How do you get a teen-aged boy to go where a mother

wants him? You might have a friend arrange for a teen-aged cheerleader to invite him.

"I'll think it over," Danny answered her, and he did, at length.

During the rushed days just before Christmas vacation, Danny and I were both weary and irritable. He talked back when I reprimanded him for watching TV although his chores were incomplete. I didn't like it at all.

I was surprised, too, for he hadn't done that in a long while and I had relaxed my discipline some. But he repeatedly talked back in the next few minutes.

I should have suggested that we talk about it at another time but proper discipline had done much for his attitudes and I knew I must continue with it whether I felt like it or not. So I resolved to be strong and as we talked the Lord gave me unexpected strength.

"If you talk back to me one more time, I'm going to start taking off *weeks* on the calendar, instead of days before you can drive your own car."

"You aren't trying to understand me," was his reply.

"The first week in March," I returned.

"You aren't listening to my side of it," he flung back.

"If you insist, I will take off months instead of weeks," was my next remark.

"Why won't you hear how I feel about it?" His voice was louder.

"April—" My heart thumped faster.

"You aren't being fair." His capable fingers turned into fists.

"May—"

"Why can't I talk?"

"June—"

He burst into tears.

"I'll leave this house," he started shouting.

I began to tremble.

"That is fine with me. Either you learn to control yourself, do as I asked, and then go to bed for the evening or I'll be happy to help you pack." Those were pretty strong words. Could I bear to see him go? I turned and went upstairs. My outward calm covered inner fear that suddenly swept over me in waves, threatening to drown me. Steady, I said to myself.

I know exactly how much was at stake. I could not let him have the upper hand. He must obey if he stayed in my house. He should not be the authority, although he did well on assuming some of the responsibility.

A few minutes later he came to my side. "I think we should talk this over."

"Danny, your college money is assured. Your home is here. Insurance money will buy your clothes, and I will feed you. You are also capable of working for these things. It wouldn't be easy, but you could do it."

"Yes, I could."

"If you prefer to leave, that's your choice. I won't send the police to find you. I am through talking. The decision is up to you." I tried to speak slowly and quietly.

At another time, with a different young man, under varying circumstances, we might have blown apart. For me, God's love and grace held us together.

He walked out. In a few minutes I heard the vacuum cleaner running in his room and I knew he was going to stay.

"Thanks, Lord," I said weakly, and went to bed.

XII

Only a widow knows how another widow feels about holidays. They are wicked times to live through, every first celebration of any special date that was shared in the past with a loved one who now exists only in memory.

I'm positive we had Christmas. I can't remember going to my folks, but I think we did. It might have been more sensible to have them visit us, to keep us off the road, and to keep us occupied preparing for company. But it was one of those times I didn't want to remember, so I guess I erased most of it from my mind.

My brother took me out on New Year's Eve after the children were in bed. I tried to be good company but my thoughts were not connected to my body or the present time at all. He understood for he had been through the same situation.

I had anticipated how I would feel on the anniversary of Charlie's death as early as the previous summer, and had arranged for three families to visit us on New Year's Day.

"Please come early, eat lunch with us, and watch football on TV all afternoon," I had urged.

They responded.

"Would you make some sticks to keep these sliding glass doors and windows tight against burglars?" I requested after lunch. It was one of the few problems in our new home.

When I asked for help, I always received it. No one ever made fun of the special fears I had as a widow. So the men who came to visit didn't just eat and watch football with their families.

Danny decided he had thought it over long enough and attended a couple of Young Life meetings during the holidays, in January, he joined one group for a weekend ski retreat in the mountains during semester break.

Right after he returned, he came and sat on the basement steps near where I was playing the piano.

"Mother, I've got a song I want you to play." He hadn't done that since Davy Crockett days, when he was five and wore a coonskin cap more than ten years ago.

"What's the name of it?"

"Things Are Different Now."

"I've never heard of it. You know I don't play well without music to read but if you'll sing it, I'll try."

The theme was, "Things are different now, something's happened to me, since I gave my heart to Jesus."

I was ecstatic! Joy filled my whole being for that was his way of letting me know that he had the greatest thing in the world, a personal relationship with the Lord.

I couldn't decide whether to laugh or cry. It was thrilling and I was happy and I wanted to shout, and I was relieved enough to use tears as a release.

Instead, I pretended to be absorbed in getting the music correct and learning the words. It was the easiest way he knew to share with me and my heart soared to new heights as we sat singing together.

My prayer that night probably made the Lord smile. It was wonderful to experience His presence in the life of my child. I met more of God's family in the months that followed, men and women who helped my son. I wasn't personally experienced enough to guide him well, and I was grateful.

As Danny attended the weekly meetings, months passed and the Lord seemed to select a Young Life leader to influence him. Like a substitute father, he helped Danny make good decisions. Will Perkins, in Colorado Springs, doesn't just sell cars. He and his wife open their home to young people and give away lots of the Lord's love.

One night in February Danny and some of his friends decided to go tobogganing and went driving into the mountains on icy roads. I tried hard not to be uneasy, reminding myself that God would take care of him, yet wanting to return to my old custom of worrying.

The telephone rang at ten.

"Hello."

"Hello, mother. This is Danny."

"Yes."

"Now don't get worried, but I've been in an accident."

Don't panic, I pleaded with myself.

"Is anyone hurt?"

"No, but the front of my car has the grill smashed and the water is leaking out."

My mind fought for control over fear. Remember the Lord is with him, I said to myself. My heart slowed its pace a little.

"What should we do?" I asked him.

"I have a ride home, and I'll park the car at the church camp. We can come back up and see about it tomorrow. Okay?"

"Yes. Thanks for calling."

"Thank you, Lord, for being there and caring for him," I prayed. "Bring him home safely." Am I really calm? I asked myself.

I needed my rest, for I had school to teach tomorrow.

The next thing I knew it was a little after eleven and Danny was knocking on my bedroom door.

"I'm home safe and everything is all right, mother." I had been truly resting in the Lord, sound asleep.

I was proud of myself, for I was learning slowly to turn my troubles over to the Lord and leave them there. God reassured me constantly with the joy of answered prayer.

During March and April I knew where Danny spent his spare time and that his friends were healthy to be with; I knew his group had a fine leader and were loved. I didn't fear the advice he would be given, or even how he would react to bad advice. And I felt that the other children would learn from him since he was the eldest.

We began to memorize Bible verses at mealtime as a family, and I was able to enjoy evenings at home with my children. I felt comforted by this togetherness.

Spring came early that year, at least in my heart.

XIII

May was a busy time. As an elementary teacher, I worked to complete records and list final grades. "I'm not certain these little checks are even valid," I commented to a fellow teacher as I finished over thirty report cards.

Daily, I found myself asking during classtime, "Is your paper complete?" Students and teachers were getting restless. Challenges capable of puncturing spring fever daydreams had to be found and issued.

It was one year past my Mother's Day weekend of tears, and very little was different as school work went. Nor had surroundings or physical habits changed, but my attitudes had and my heart was happier.

After school hours, I searched for a deeper meaning of the Scriptures to apply to my life. As the pastor taught God's rules for living and the Sunday school teacher pointed out the personal nature of Christ's relationship with others, I remembered my past. Experiences with people from other years were dovetailed into my current listening and helped me understand the human nature pictured in stories from the life of Christ. His interaction with people became important to me. I would be able to look back in future years with little regret if I followed his example.

Gradually, I tried on the garments of God's grace. One at a time I learned of and accepted more of His promises to me, as His child. I was trying to do my share and just watching to see what He would complete in the lives of my children. I knew it would take time, but would be significant for their happiness as well as mine.

Pleased with my own adjustment, I made a new decision. I wanted my body, as God's living place, to be free of unnecessary medications. I was grateful that God had given doctors the ability to provide me with relief, but I felt that sleeping pills and tranquilizers must now be put aside.

"I'm going to stop all the pills today," I said to my physician in June.

"You can't do that abruptly; you'll have to taper off," he said.

"Just watch!"

I believed that God would help me. In return for my belief he gave me peaceful sleep with very few nightmares and the ability to discuss Charlie's death with calmness. That immediate answer to my prayer caused me to depend increasingly on him and to be even more certain of his love as summer days passed.

I knew God loved me, but how nice to be reminded! Growing in faith, I found myself turning over to him areas of my life that I had unknowingly withheld. I admitted all fears and asked his guidance. How would I spend my spare time wisely beyond guiding the children? I questioned as I quietly talked to him. How could I learn to tell others of the glory of his love? And he seemed to say, "Study and be patient. Heal. The time will come."

I had to remind myself repeatedly not to take back what I had given to him, not to allow worry about my own future. It was his. I need not push. It might take time to learn his wishes, but he would lead.

I decided to practice relaxing, being joyful, and enjoying the present *not* just a day at a time, but expectantly looking for pleasure in the future. My ability to do exactly that grew with practice.

The passage of time was part of his natural healing process, but I had rebelled earlier about waiting. I had wanted to be adjusted to the new situation right then.

"Hurry! Mother!" my children repeated a word I had used with them for years. It was pleasing to realize that I had now changed my pace and could say to them, "Why hurry?"

I became willing to walk slowly, more able to appreciate the surrounding beauty as I surmounted each foothill.

Little frustrations were always present, but they were lessened when I remembered that God was in control and would guide me into the future. I no longer had to fight my way forward on my own ahead of him.

As a new widow I had been numb, in shock and unaware of others, overly concerned with my own feelings. Now I found it possible to see beyond my reactions, even past the adjustment of my children, to our society, as individuals and as a group.

Many of my former friends were uncomfortable around me, not knowing what to do or say. I was no help to them either. What could I tell them? I didn't know how to express the fact that all I really needed was their love, acceptance, and presence, or that it wasn't necessary for a person to speak particular words.

I appreciated the shared experiences of older widows. I could ask them questions without fear of being laughed at, such as, "What do you do about sex?" My group of friends began to change.

If I were visiting a widow who was just beginning her adjustment to widowhood I might hear, "I just came from my lawyer's office where I made out a will." We would chuckle together, because a will inevitably seemed vital to new widows.

Some women, perhaps unconsciously, didn't want me near. Many wives, insecure in their own marriages, believed my main desire was to steal their partner, not realizing that I still mourned the loss of Charlie. They just didn't understand.

"I don't want your husband. I want my own," I wanted to tell them, but I didn't. They were fearful and wouldn't have heard or believed. It became more and more uncomfortable around ordinary couples. There were some who understood me, mostly those involved in second marriages with some aspect of experience that correlated with mine.

It took a great amount of courage to go anywhere as a single parent with children, but I still couldn't resist attending a family retreat. It was an opportunity to drive up into my beloved mountains. Just the scenery would have made it worthwhile but there were a couple of other surprises.

When we walked into the large family style dining room a momentary desire overtook me. Escape! Did I belong here? without a mate? Would the Sunday school members be friendly away from class since they hardly knew me?

"Will you sit with us?" a couple immediately invited us to their table.

I breathed a sigh of relief and sat down. "I'm a widow and don't have a partner," I said inanely. I wanted to set the record straight right away.

"I was widowed and responsible for three boys for twelve years before I met and married Shelton," Jean confided moments later. We had a fine visit for she understood all my present emotions.

Shelton's hobby was mechanics so he advised me on some work needed on Danny's used car. I should have known—the Lord was ahead of me again.

The children splashed in the pool and galloped on horseback along mountain paths, while I basked in God's love from his Word, his people, and his world of nature.

Our speaker for the weekend walked beside the children and me as we strolled down the valley to the chuck wagon for breakfast the next morning. I found myself telling him of my moods and emotions as a widow. His friendliness soon pulled from deep within me my secret wish.

"I want to be a writer," I confessed, "but I'm busy teaching school."

"Keep a diary or journal. Put your ideas down and send them to me later if you ever find time. I'll critique your work," he encouraged.

So fuel was added to the spark as he helped light the way. Another of God's children willing to help me. They seem to be everywhere!

Time after time God sent someone to meet my current need, to offer advice, or to encourage me. He smoothed the pathway and helped me climb upward.

My strides grew longer—I could see the view from a

higher perspective. Less depression . . . more will to live . . . joy that would bubble over into genuine laughter influencing the lives of my children. My Lord did anything I believed he would if it brought glory to himself.

There was depth to his teaching and I wanted to learn more. I tried to keep close to him in study, unselfish living, and serious prayer. One of my favorite hymns, "What a Friend We Have in Jesus" developed an additional meaning. He is *my* friend!

I found him a natural part of my life. If a day passed and I felt something was missing, upon considering it, I realized—it was a day without devotion time. As my body required food, so my spirit needed his Word.

I found myself singing as I moved through my daily schedule, and my children began to be more playful. We were ready to do something relaxing.

XIV

Charlie's folks had worked hard rearing a large family through the depression years. Mine had given time in teaching, church activities, and public service organizations. Both sets of parents had done without luxury to lend us college funds.

So, as a sort of memorial to Charlie, thinking that it would have pleased him, I planned to take the four grandparents to Hawaii. I knew nothing about planning the details of such a trip, and wouldn't have tried as a lone widow, but a travel agent listened to my desires and she totally planned flights, motels, and inter-island travel. I hadn't known such service was available and would never have guessed it cost nothing.

"I will fly anywhere, as long as I can keep one foot on the ground," my daddy had said earlier, but the grandparents were gracious receivers and all agreed to travel by air. It was a big decision, flying, for each of us.

Hawaii was predominantly green, but rainbow country. Flowers bloomed everywhere. "Orchids grow wild," I kept repeating. Blossoms were so thick on some flowering trees that there appeared to be no leaves.

I took colorful slides of each parent with a flower lei. Having to purchase our leis was my only disappointment during the whole trip. Being my usual naive self, I had expected someone to greet us and present us each with one, *free!*

We rented a car and toured three islands. Near Hilo, a sleepy volcano steadily puffed smoke out at us from cracks in the earth. We were tempted to try walking through the acres of rough, cutting lava boulders that we drove past on our way around the lower end of one island. They reminded me of giant coal clinkers like the small ones Charlie and I had taken from the bottom of the old coal stove in western Colorado.

I took slides showing pineapple fields, moving in closer and closer to the plants on the ground, until we had one tilted-over ripe pineapple alone in a slide. I planned to make a tape and talk about these slides in my third grade classroom.

The huge fields were free of weeds. Long rolls of tar paper had been put down, with spaced holes for the plants. A man walked along irrigating small pineapple plants from a water bag over his shoulder. He seemed out of place compared to the large modern yellow machines used to pick and sort the fruit in other fields.

We cut a sugar cane stalk from a field filled with thick, long rows of plants that were over our heads. We sliced little circles of it to chew. Enormous sprayers were watering with pulsating, strong spurts, high and wide over the fields, using dirty water from a ditch.

I was upset that the rice fields we were directed to turned out to be taro growing, but the peaceful valley view we saw from the top of the incline looking out to the ocean was worth the drive. We kept seeing large, filled gunny sacks beside the road. We decided it was some type of vegetable.

"I want to see what is in those," Charlie's dad said. I stopped the car. But when he looked, he still didn't know.

"I'm going to taste one of these," he said next. He took a slice off the end of one and got back into the car. I wasn't bold enough to taste it.

"My mouth is burning and I've already swallowed some," he said as we drove on.

He began to complain so we stopped at a small grocery store along the country road for some milk.

"What is in the sacks beside the road?" he asked a native clerk, but she couldn't seem to understand him.

"Poi—" she said and stopped.

"I thought she was trying to say poison but couldn't," he solemnly told us later. "I was pretty frightened for a few minutes."

She finally made him understand that he had tasted a taro root from which poi is made.

We all had a good laugh, and he finally chuckled with us. It reminded me of Charlie, for he was constantly smelling and tasting things when he was alive, even other people's medicine, just out of curiosity. It was a warm memory.

We reminisced about Charlie a short while. It was comforting, rather than upsetting. I knew I was healing because I was able to talk about him and show love to others who had cared for him instead of crying. Time was helping.

We didn't have one missing bag, weren't late for one plane, and didn't have one ounce of energy left. I decided the Lord had approved and watched over each detail of our time schedule. I asked him to bless our relatives who cared for a total of eight youngsters counting mine, in California, while we were gone.

We distributed grass leis and skirts to sunburned children when we reached the mainland. "Now, you all line up and give us a hula dance," I suggested. They did.

We had a fun time sharing a day in Disneyland before we flew home for restful summer days.

One by one, the children attended church camp. Danny grew spiritually. He brought home pictures of himself near the lake with the Young Life group in Minnesota.

Kathy came home with questions about her daddy and eternity. It was as if she were considering the same things I had wondered about a year previously, or had we just progressed to the point where we could talk about it at last? I was glad I had studied and found answers.

Ruthy came home with understanding beyond her years, and a renewed love for others. "I have a new Friend, mother," was her greeting.

Paul David took a boyfriend with him. Between times of catching frogs near the pond and hiking in the woods, he had heard a story which impressed him.

"There's going to be a time when Christ comes back to earth, mom."

"Really?"

"Yes, and some people are going to go and live with him!"

"Is that right?"

"Yes."

Paul David had been more than a little bit frightened. "I didn't want to be left behind, so I asked Christ to be my Lord and Savior," he continued.

"I'm glad, Paul David," I said and smiled at him. He couldn't have known how truly pleased I was, for it meant that each of my four children shared the Lord with me.

I wondered if the story were a scare tactic, like earlier days of preaching too much hell and damnation, but I wasn't prepared to make an issue of it. I pondered about it in my mind and decided that maybe it takes something dramatic to teach American men and boys. We teach them to be so independent that it is nearly impossible for them to admit they need to rely on anyone, even God the Father.

As Paul David dumped his dirty clothes on the floor beside the washer I noticed his new jeans. He hadn't torn off the pockets! "Thanks, Lord, that he feels worthy to wear new clothes again," was my immediate silent prayer. And I was able to thank him for many large and small blessings as my second summer as a widow came to a close.

I drove to and from school during autumn of 1968 allowing the contrast of the golden aspen leaves throughout the green spruce to delight me. Similar to the color and variety in my life—helps keep it interesting—I thought.

XV

That fall I tried singing solos for the Sunday night congregation. It wasn't easy to do alone and without Charlie, but the words of many songs seemed to express my "before and after" feeling about knowing Christ in a more personal way. Singing would be one way to let others know how I felt since I couldn't seem to talk much about it yet.

I sang once. By the end of the first verse my mouth was dry. I couldn't possibly continue.

I glanced at the pastor. His head was bowed, obviously praying. For me?

I frantically sought the face of his wife at the piano. She looked up. Would she understand? I took hold of the pedestal in front of me for support. She nodded her head, and even though we hadn't planned it, she played an extra chorus while I managed to moisten my mouth. I finished in a wavering voice, but I did finish.

I sang again. This Sunday night the pastor's wife played all over the keyboard and in between verses while I read, "Lo, I am with you always," silently to myself. I had written it at the top of my music.

"Why don't you put clappers on your knees and sing 'Jingle Bells'?" my daddy teased at Christmas time when we went to visit my folks. I could have accompanied myself that way, for my wobbly knees still trembled some even then when I sang. We had a merry time anyway.

Singing became easier as I kept trying, and best if I sang frequently. It was a traumatic experience each time for months. But I persisted, for I hoped that in the future it would become easy. When I knew his people were praying for me, it helped.

Each of my children was adjusting at his or her own speed and their pathways were sometimes rocky, too.

Ruthy had advanced to junior high. Too many students for limited space had resulted in three shifts a day. When the rest of us went to school each day, Ruthy had two hours to be alone since she attended the third group.

I noticed she was becoming more reluctant to get out of bed each day of the new year.

"What's the matter?" I asked.

"There's a girl hitting me and chasing me every day!"

Finally she admitted that she had been mistreated by another student who boosted her own ego by boasting of how she tormented others. And she didn't boast about what she didn't do!

The teasing was tough and Ruthy's two hours alone each morning gave her time to mentally enlarge trouble. I could pick her up after school during dark winter evenings, but I was teaching in the morning.

Counselors and the school nurse tried to help, but

the situation didn't improve. My way of life now consisted of doing all I could about every aspect of our lives and trustingly turning over to the Lord the things that were beyond my fingertips. I couldn't think of any solution for Ruthy's problem so I asked him specifically for an answer.

The Lord works through human beings. Soon help came through a teacher who taught down the hall from me.

"Why don't you let Ruthy come to school with you in the morning?" she asked.

"I wouldn't feel right about doing that. The principal might think I'm trying to take advantage of the situation," I replied.

"I can and I will," she said. So Ruthy helped with Edna's primary reading circle each morning and I took her to her own classes during my lunch hour. Gradually, she relaxed, and I was soon able to say, "Thanks, again, Lord!" I knew he understood that I was talking about Ruthy having overcome her lifelong habit of biting her nails.

In an effort to spend more time with the children I secretly took ski lessons at the Broadmoor. I'm not fond of cold air, so it was a sacrifice on my part but I had more energy than usual. I wasn't a star student. When we practiced getting off the ski lift at the top, it was one of the most frightening experiences of my life. However, it was worth the astounded look on the faces of my children when I informed them just before spring vacation that I was going skiing with them.

"Mother, you can't just take off and ski. You have to have lessons," Kathy said. The children had learned to ski a year earlier.

"Oh, I've had lessons! You'll see when we get to the slopes," I said.

It was pleasant, riding up to the top of Buttermilk Mountain, the gentlest slope around Aspen. The beauty of the view enveloped me. Topside, the snow on other jagged ridges, the blanketed white trees, and the sunshine reflecting from a rainbow of ski jackets made me feel like I was in the middle of a rainbow. I could have stayed up there all day and enjoyed it tremendously. And should have!

The children were encouraging at first.

"Come on, mother, this is a gentle slope!" Danny urged, and away he skiied, an effortless and smooth glide.

"You can do it mother. I'll go right ahead of you. See how easy it is." Ruthy started down. She turned at the first curve to wait and watch.

"Are you certain this is the beginner's slope?" I was feeling quivery inside. Talk about tense muscles.

"You go ahead mother. I'll follow you to be sure you are okay," Paul David comforted me in a soft voice.

"I'll ski right beside you mother, so you'll have company," Kathy quietly assured me.

But in less than thirty minutes, they all wailed in agreed exasperation. "Mother, you aren't supposed to sit down on every turn!"

Needing more ability than I possessed from my limited four-lesson experience, I spent the whole afternoon skiing down once (I even hesitate as I call it skiing), and my new interest halted at the bottom of the hill. My first view from the top was my first and my last. Too old to learn?

I would just stay where I could be more safe, I decided. Why bother to ask God for more courage if I didn't really want it?

Easter came and this time I was able to sing in the choir, sharing in the excitement of special music. I was filled with expectancy regarding eternal life, and joyful about the Lord's daily presence.

We walked out of the service at noon. Huge, billowing, white clouds reached miles into the heavens.

"I think the Lord could step right out of a cloud like that one!" I said, pointing for the children. "Wouldn't it be wonderful if he came today?"

"Great! . . . Let's go eat," Danny replied.

As I drove toward town, I reflected on the recent years of adjustment. It's a grand view from the top of the valley, I thought. I looked ahead and upward.

BIBLIOGRAPHY

Westberg, Granger. *Good Grief*. Fortress Press.